Lovers and Tramps

Nick Monks

Bluebell Publishing

For Amanda, Karl, Saskia

Title Page

Lovers and Tramps- Nick Monks

Published July 2020

Printed by Lulu

www.lulu.com

ISBN : 978-1-8381263-0-8

CONTENTS

Lovers and Tramps

Lovers 1

They spent 4 years together
In a cottage in the Cotswolds
Then one morning she left

He remembers her for 20 years
Through attrition, strife and bleak torpor
Always he awaits her tap on the door
Her approaching him through a crowded high street
Her letter to him
Her beckoning by a silver moors stream.

Tramps 1

It is raining in Bristol's outlying villages
Barnabas hasn't eaten for three days
And to avoid the unforgiving long tarmac roads
He traipses through a field
The clayey mud cakes and sticks to his £7 plimsoles
The rain is also unforgiving and soaks through the kagool
To his jumper. And his jeans abrade the skin from his thighs
On the other side of the field
The other side of the long road
The other side of the Severn estuary
The other side of the Mendip's
Is Annwn, it is vital to avoid the city. The goal is so near.

Lovers 2

The lover of Keith is back from Iraq
He sighs in relief
It's not his nurses wife's TLC they were after
And their days resume their routines
He waited a year for the loss to repair.

Tramps 2

The tramp gets £30 together
He's sleeping under a bridge in Avondale park Preston
Treads across town to go to the opera
In the foyer
A group usurp his table
Were he sits sipping a lime and soda
He joins in the conversation
"I like Wilde he's so witty" says the man
"It's all Avatar Avatar, and Transformers on in the cinema"
Says the woman
In the theatre listening to Bellini's Norma
He sips his drink
The oh so sophisticated opera audience rouse
And cat call at the final curtain call
The tramp goes back to the bridge in the park
With Wittgenstein's *Philosophical Investigations*
Read under the park path lamp
As the kids taunt him and shout "hobo hobo."

Lovers 3

After 10 years of travelling and working abroad
He goes after arriving at Dover
Straight hitching along the coastal path
To Eastbourne. Walks to the entrance to the flat door
Knocks as if it were ordained.

There is no answer. He sits on the steps
Gazes at the grey clouded sky. Seagulls pass
There he hears her voice sees her vicariously
Walks away to continue travelling in Britain.

Tramps 3

At Roscoff the silver liner ship, is-
Pulling away from the wharf. He cannot board
Late. He buys a ticket for tomorrows sailing

Asks the night security can he sleep on the floor of the
terminal
Waits for the suns rise over Le Manche. Beckoning.

Lovers 4

All night the red sea waves crashed uncharacteristically
On the fine white sand of Eilat beach
The westerners took shelter in hotel doorways
When the tempest was over. The beach had gone
But Fiona remained tracing finger prints on a Brighton-
Frosted window pane.

Tramps 4

When the tramp arrives in Calais he only has 15 euros
So Barabas walks through Calais west
Shoreward is a beach. A ship turning there towards Dover
He walks for four days
Hostile to flickers of gesture from passers-by
Past the Germans fortifications.
Inland to cross two rivers
Sleeping where he fell on the sand. Collecting cigarette butts
From the coastal towns passed through

The final river was too difficult to cross. He treads to Amiens
Has money now. Sleeps in a hotel. Stays in Beauvais
Were Joan of Arc was tried. Heads reluctantly to Paris
Regrets the termination of the coastal walk. Halted by a
wide river on the Baie de la Somme.

Lovers 5

When in Hull at University. He looses the thread of Fiona
The telephone call that went badly.
After two hours wandering Hulls streets in trepidation
His life expands to admit the foreign. And thus chaos eats
away at his limbs.

Tramps 5

In London residents put railings to prevent tramps sleeping
Away from Victoria station Barnabas finds a doorway
And sleeps, the icy air wistfully playing on the sleeping bags
slumber
Tomorrow the national express coach will take him to
Preston
Britain's harshness after the Black Forest/the Vosges/
Hungary/Austria/Brussels/Liege/

Lovers 6

Snow became. Rhiannon's touch. Waiting. Ice particles
Frozen fingertips. Dressage of symphonies. Wars refugees.
Barren neighbours who shout. Thousands of windows
boarded up. Rhiannon walking on the estuary at night.

Tramps 6

Barnabas has walked through the Lairig Ghru pass
Through the Cairngorms
In Aviemore he waits for the passers-by's to go,
on the bench arranges the sleeping bag
Registers the moving light, shadow on the crag
The cold clear air. Oystercatchers over- head calling.

Lovers 7

In Shenzhen from the hotel you walk
Every 50 meters a girl approaches
You think there saying "pizza pizza"
You think "great I have not eaten for five days, were?"
Back at the hotel with five girls in the lift
And no help from the hotel staff
You realize they were saying "me sir, me sir"
You gaze at the hotel receptionist
Hoping she will say. "Just ignore them love"
But the receptionist are impeccably dressed
And there is not a flicker of anything scrutable in their faces
Perhaps they are saying. "what's wrong with you have you
no money"

In the morning catching the train to Hong Kong
You feel no change in self. A little happier. But no collapses
Or change. I guess this is China not Bristol or Bordeaux.

Tramps 7

Malaysia

The boat to Singapore to Indonesia took 12 hours
So with an 11pm boarding in Indonesia
For the return crossing. Anda wider sea
There was no need to save money
Tomorrow was paty day
But the ship was fast very- It took 5 hours

In Penang at 4am
You look about, seedy faces glare out from doorways
The first four ATM'S say "insufficient funds"
The forth gives you just enough for cigarettes
A drink and a hotel room. That was close.

Lovers 8

She was so beautiful. She tore up your rule book
Left you tattered and in a diaspora of the mind.

Tramps 8

After a night of them not me drinking
The only one of you with money pays for the taxi
And at Malaga airport. You sleep
But cannot afford a plane to Gatwick.

Lovers 9

Branwen the Celt left you untouched. So in this poem I leave her unwritten about. So she may be radiant and whole. And untouched untainted. A before. Like a sea baptism.

Tramps 9

When you can't find the key, you walk to a park-
In Hull wait for the next day in a bench shelter
At 2am a lad joins you. He's also locked out
The sejourner devours you inwardly. Even when your back in
The bedsit the next day after your landlord arrives.

Lovers 10

For 30 years he hasn't seen
Or heard from she

But he awaits her
Each day she watches over him
It is only a matter of trivial time.

Tramps 10

Tramps sleep in door ways
And tell themselves its alright

They sit in subways awaiting
Begged for pound coins
Do not pass by these lovers
Listen to the harmonica drop in a
Five pound note

It will be cold in the sleeping bag tonight.

www.ingramcontent.com/pod-product-compliance
Lightning Source LLC
Chambersburg PA
CBHW021948040426
42448CB00008B/1303